PEANUTS
GUIDE TO LIFE

Book 1

By Charles M. Schulz

ℛℛ
RAVETTE PUBLISHING

This edition published by Ravette Publishing 2007.

ISBN 978-1-84161-268-3

CONTENTS

Peanuts Guide to:

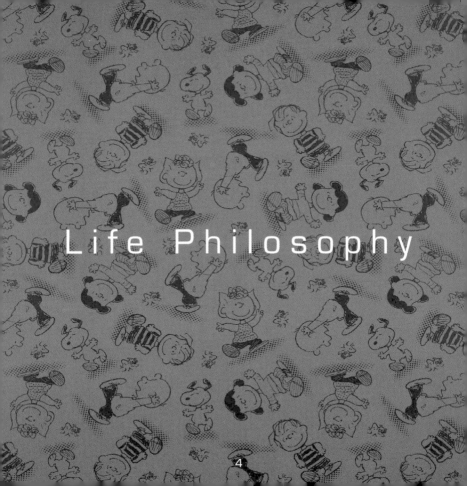

Life Philosophy

"LIFE IS LIKE AN ICE CREAM CONE. . .
YOU HAVE TO LEARN TO LICK IT!"

Charlie Brown

"AS SOON AS A CHILD IS BORN,
HE OR SHE SHOULD BE ISSUED
WITH A DOG AND A BANJO. . ."

Charlie Brown

"THEY SAY IF YOU BECOME
A BETTER PERSON, YOU'LL HAVE
A BETTER LIFE..."

Charlie Brown

"IF YOU TRY TO BE A BETTER DOG,
SOMETIMES YOU GET AN
EXTRA COOKIE. . ."

Snoopy

"I HAVE A PHILOSOPHY THAT HAS BEEN REFINED IN THE FIRES OF HARDSHIP AND STRUGGLE. . . 'LIVE AND LET LIVE!'"

Lucy

"A LIFE SHOULD BE PLANNED
INNING BY INNING."

Peppermint Patty

Wisdom

"I HAVE OBSERVED THAT WHENEVER
YOU TRY TO HIT SOMEBODY, THERE IS
A TENDENCY FOR THEM TO
TRY TO HIT YOU BACK."

Charlie Brown

"WHENEVER IT'S ONE MAN AGAINST
AN INSTITUTION, THERE IS ALWAYS A
TENDENCY FOR THE INSTITUTION TO WIN!"

Charlie Brown

"NEVER TRY TO LICK ICE CREAM
OFF A HOT SIDEWALK!"

Snoopy

"NEVER TAKE ANY ADVICE THAT YOU
CAN UNDERSTAND. . . IT CAN'T POSSIBLY
BE ANY GOOD!"

Lucy

"NEVER JUMP INTO A PILE OF LEAVES
HOLDING A WET SUCKER!"

Linus

Self-Reliance

"IF YOU WANT SOMETHING DONE RIGHT,
YOU SHOULD DO IT YOURSELF!"

Snoopy

"WELL FROM NOW ON, LINUS,
THINK FOR YOURSELF. . . DON'T TAKE
ANY ADVICE FROM ANYONE!"

Charlie Brown

"WHO CARES WHAT OTHER PEOPLE THINK?"

Sally

"YOU CAN'T BELIEVE EVERYTHING
YOU HEAR, YOU KNOW. . ."

Schroeder

Other PEANUTS Gift Books available ...

	ISBN	Price
A Friend is ... forever	978-1-84161-213-3	£4.99
Best Friends ... understand sharing	978-1-84161-258-4	£4.99
Happiness is ... a warm puppy	978-1-84161-211-9	£4.99
Love is ... walking hand in hand	978-1-84161-212-6	£4.99
Peanuts Guide to Life Book 2	978-1-84161-269-0	£4.99
Peanuts Guide to Life Book 3	978-1-84161-287-4	£4.99
Security is ... a thumb and a blanket	978-1-84161-210-2	£4.99
True Love is ... complete trust	978-1-84161-259-1	£4.99

HOW TO ORDER   Please send a cheque/postal order in £ sterling, made payable to 'Ravette Publishing' for the cover price of the books and allow the following for post & packaging ...

UK & BFPO	70p for the first book & 40p per book thereafter
Europe & Eire	£1.30 for the first book & 70p per book thereafter
Rest of the world	£2.20 for the first book & £1.10 per book thereafter

RAVETTE PUBLISHING LTD
Unit 3 Tristar Centre, Star Road, Partridge Green, West Sussex RH13 8RA
Tel: 01403 711443   Fax: 01403 711554   Email: ravettepub@aol.com